SCIENTIFIC AMERICAN. EDUCATIONAL PUBLISHING

PUSH AND PULL

10 FUN

EXPERIMENTS WITH FORCES

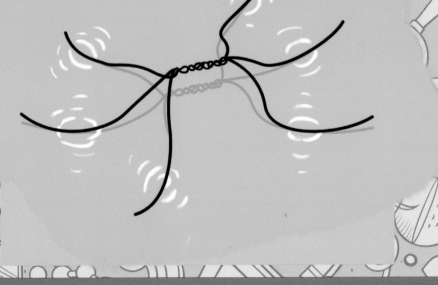

BRING SCIENCE HOME

Published in 2024 by The Rosen Publishing Group, Inc.
2544 Clinton Street, Buffalo, NY 14224

Contains material from Scientific American , a division of Springer Nature America, Inc., reprinted by permission as well as original material from The Rosen Publishing Group.

Editor: Kristen Rajczak Nelson
Designer: Rachel Rising

Activity on p. 5 by Science Buddies, Ben Finio (September 8, 2016); p. 9 by Science Buddies (February 23, 2012); p. 15 by Science Buddies, Ben Finio (July 26, 2018); p. 21 by Science Buddies, Ben Finio (November 29, 2018); p. 27 by Science Buddies (February 28, 2013); p. 33 by Science Buddies, Ben Finio (October 22, 2015); p. 37 by Science Buddies (February 26, 2015); p. 43 by Science Buddies (September 4, 2014); p. 49 Science Buddies (July 30, 2015); p. 55 by Science Buddies (October 10, 2013).

All illustrations by Continuum Content Solutions

Photo Credits: pp. 5, 9, 15, 21, 27, 33, 37, 43, 49, 55 Anna Frajtova/Shutterstock.com; pp. 5, 7, 9, 1,2, 21, 24, 27, 29, 30, 37, 40, 43, 46, 55, 57 cve iv/Shutterstock.com.

Cataloging-in-Publication Data
Names: Scientific American, Inc.
Title: Push and pull: 10 fun experiments with forces / edited by the Scientific American Editors.
Description: New York : Scientific American Educational Publishing, an imprint of Rosen Publishing, 2024. | Series: Bring science home | Includes glossary and index.
Identifiers: ISBN 9781725350038 (pbk.) | ISBN 9781725350045 (library bound) | ISBN 9781725350052 (ebook)
Subjects: LCSH: Force and energy--Experiments--Juvenile literature.
Classification: LCC QC73.4 P87 2024 | DDC 531'.6078--dc23

Manufactured in the United States of America

CPSIA Compliance Information: Batch #CWSA24. For further information contact Rosen Publishing, New York, New York at 1-800-237-9932.

Find us on

CONTENTS

THESE ACTIVITIES INCLUDE
SCIENCE FAIR PROJECT IDEAS.

INTRODUCTION

Did you know there's a science to the swing you play on during recess? Or the yo-yo you play with? Forces are all around us all the time. They allow us to walk, play, work, and simply live. Learn more about forces and physics in the following activities!

Projects marked with  include a section called Science Fair Project Ideas. These ideas can help you develop your own original science fair project. Science fair judges tend to reward creative thought and imagination, and it helps if you are really interested in your project. You will also need to follow the scientific method. See page 61 for more information about that.

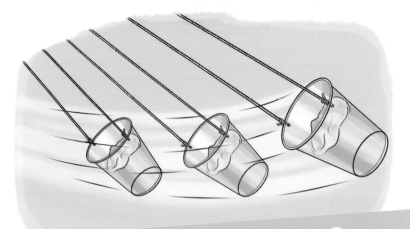

Gravity-Defying Water

CAN YOU FLIP A CUP OF WATER WITHOUT GETTING WET? USE A LITTLE PHYSICS, AND GIVE THIS EXPECTATION-BENDING ACTIVITY A SPIN!

Can you turn a cup of water upside-down without the water pouring out? Sounds impossible, right? This project will show you how you can do it using a neat physics trick!

PROJECT TIME
15 to 20 minutes

KEY CONCEPTS
Physics
Gravity
Inertia
Centripetal force

BACKGROUND

Have you ever gone around a fast curve while riding in a car? Did you notice how it feels like you are being "pushed" to the outside of the curve? You are not actually being pushed—rather, your body "wants" to continue traveling in a straight line. (This is called inertia.) Your seat belt and the friction of the seat against your body pull you along with the car as it turns, however. This force that makes your body turn instead of continuing to go straight is called centripetal force.

So, that works when you go around a horizontal curve in a car. What happens if you go through a vertical curve, such as a roller coaster loop? On a roller coaster, all riders are strapped in for extra safety. There are plenty of examples where things go through vertical loops without being strapped in—such as a toy race car or marble on a track. What prevents them from falling down at the top of the loop? The same concepts apply. The toy car has inertia because it is moving, so it "wants" to keep moving in a straight line. The curved track pushes on the car's tires (providing a centripetal force), however, forcing it to move in a loop instead of going straight. If the car is moving fast enough, it will speed through the loop without ever losing contact with the track. If it is going too slowly, it will not have enough inertia and it will fall before it makes it through the loop.

It turns out that you can also apply this exact same concept to liquids! If you fill a cup with water and tie it to a string, you can spin the cup around in a horizontal or vertical circle. As long as you spin it fast enough, the water will not spill out! Still don't believe it? Try the procedure below to prove it to yourself!

MATERIALS

- Paper or plastic cup
- String
- Scissors
- Water

PREPARATION

- Find an outdoor area where it is okay if you spill a little water. Make sure there are no people or objects nearby that you could hit when twirling the cup.

PROCEDURE

- Carefully poke (or have an adult poke) two holes opposite each other near the top rim of the cup.

- Cut a piece of string about as long as you are tall.

- Tightly tie one end of the string to each hole in the cup to form a long handle.

- Fill the cup about halfway with water.

- Go outside to an area where it's okay if you spill a little water and where you will not hit any nearby people or objects while twirling the cup.

- Start twirling the cup over your head in a horizontal circle (so the cup moves parallel to the ground). *How fast do you need to spin it to keep the water in the cup?*

- Gradually transition to twirling the cup in a vertical circle. *Does the water stay in the cup, even at the top of the loop?*

- If the water spills out of your cup, refill it, and try again. Make sure you twirl the cup faster this time. You can also fill it with less water if you continue having trouble.

EXTRA

Try the activity with solid objects instead of liquid. *What happens if you put a toy in the cup?*

SCIENCE FAIR IDEA

Try changing the length of the string. *Does making the string longer (or shorter) make it easier or harder to keep the water in the cup?*

OBSERVATIONS AND RESULTS ··········

As long as you only fill the cup about halfway, you should be able to twirl the cup in a horizontal circle and then transition to a vertical one without spilling any water. It can be difficult to go directly to a vertical circle because the cup might not be going fast enough on the first loop to prevent water from spilling out. If you fill the cup with too much water, it can also be difficult to prevent some spillage.

CLEANUP ····················
Pour out the water, recycle the cup, and return the other materials to where you found them.

⚛ Swinging with a Pendulum

LEARN HOW PENDULUMS CAN SHOW THE EFFECTS OF EARTH'S GRAVITY ON OBJECTS WITH THIS SWINGING ACTIVITY!

PROJECT TIME

 30 to 45 minutes

KEY CONCEPTS

Physics
Gravity
Motion
Pendulums

Did you know that playground swings can provide a good lesson in physics—as well as lots of fun? The back-and-forth motion of a swing is an example of a pendulum. We see pendulums in other areas of our lives as well, such as in grandfather (also known as longcase) clocks. But pendulums can do more than provide fun at recess and help tell the time—among other scientific applications, they can show that Earth is huge! This is because the swinging motion of a pendulum is due to the force of gravity generated by Earth's size. Other factors, including a pendulum's length, can also affect its motion.

9

BACKGROUND

A pendulum is an object hung from a fixed point that swings back and forth under the action of gravity. In the example of the playground swing, the swing is supported by chains that are attached to fixed points at the top of the swing set. When the swing is raised and released, it will move freely back and forth due to the force of gravity on it. The swing continues moving back and forth without any extra outside help until friction (between the air and the swing and between the chains and the attachment points) slows it down and eventually stops it.

The time it takes a pendulum to swing back to its original position is called the period of the pendulum. For example, this is the time it takes a child being pushed in a swing to be pushed and then return back for another push. The period of the pendulum depends on the force of gravity, as well as the length of the pendulum.

MATERIALS

- Two identical chairs
- String or yarn
- Ten metal washers of identical size or six pennies
- Strong tape
- Yard stick
- Scissors
- Stopwatch accurate to 0.1 second
- An assistant

PREPARATION

- Place the two chairs back-to-back. Space them about 3 feet (0.9 m) apart. Lay the yard stick on the backs of the two chairs, centered on the back of each.

- Cut one piece of string to a length of 28 inches (71 cm). Cut a second piece of string to a length of 14 inches (36 cm). Tie one end of both strings to the yard stick, toward the middle of the stick. Space the strings about 8 to 12 inches (20 to 30.5 cm) apart on the yard stick.

- Tie five metal washers to the free end of each string. Alternatively, if you are using pennies and tape, securely tape three pennies to the free end of each string.

- **Tip:** If the yard stick does not seem to stably sit on the backs of the chairs, you can try to tape the ends of the yard stick to the chairs.

PROCEDURE •

- Pull the strings tight (by holding on to the washers or pennies at the ends) and position the strings at the same angle from the yard stick.

- Have an assistant ready with a stopwatch. Drop the longer pendulum and, at the same time, have the assistant start the stopwatch. Then have the assistant stop the stopwatch when the pendulum returns back to its original position. If the pendulum hit anything as it swung, such as the wall, readjust your setup and try timing the pendulum again. *How long does it take the longer pendulum to swing back to its original position?* This is the period of the pendulum.

- Again, pull the strings tight, and hold them at the same angle from the yard stick.

- Have the assistant reset the stopwatch. Drop the shorter pendulum and, once more, have the assistant time the period of the pendulum. *How long does it take the shorter pendulum to swing back to its original position?*

- Time the periods of the shorter and longer pendulums a few more times. *Are the periods consistent for each pendulum, or do they vary a lot?*

- *Is the period of the longer pendulum longer or shorter than the period of the shorter pendulum? How different are the two periods? Is this what you expected?*

11

OBSERVATIONS AND RESULTS ··········

Did the longer pendulum have a longer period than the shorter pendulum? Was the longer pendulum's period not quite twice as long as the shorter pendulum's period?

A pendulum's period is related to its length, but the relationship is not linear. A pendulum that is twice as long as another pendulum does not simply have a period that is also twice as long. The exact periods of your longer and shorter pendulums may be slightly less than 1.7 seconds and 1.2 seconds, respectively, because of friction and because their lengths were less than 28 inches (71 cm) and 14 inches (35.6 cm) (due to strings being used to tie to attachments).

Perhaps the most famous pendulum is Foucault's pendulum, which showed Earth's rotation in the mid-1800s. One of the first known pendulum uses was in about 100 CE when a Chinese scientist, Zhang Heng, used it to detect distant earthquakes in a device called a seismograph. Today pendulums have many applications, including measuring local gravity and helping guide ships and aircrafts.

Paper Roller Coasters

DO THE LOOP-DE-LOOP WITH PHYSICS—AND BUILD
YOUR OWN ROLLER COASTER!

Have you ever ridden a roller coaster? Have you ever wanted to design your own? There are plenty of expensive toys and even video games that will let you build your own coasters—but in this project you'll make one out of paper and tape and learn about roller coaster physics along the way!

PROJECT TIME
1 to 3 hours

KEY CONCEPTS
Physics
Gravity
Potential energy
Kinetic energy
Friction
Conservation of energy

BACKGROUND

Roller coasters are all about physics! Unlike other vehicles, such as cars and trains, roller coaster cars do not have an engine that propels them. Instead they rely on gravitational potential energy, which they gain by initially being towed up a large hill. (There are other kinds of potential energy, such as elastic potential energy, which is the kind you get when you stretch a rubber band. This project will be referring just to gravitational potential energy.)

Potential energy is "stored" because of an object's elevation or height off the ground. When the coaster car starts going down the hill, the potential energy is converted into kinetic energy, or the energy of motion. When the coaster car goes back up another hill, it will lose kinetic energy (slow down) and gain some potential energy again. Some of that is also converted to heat due to air resistance and friction with the track, gradually causing the coaster to slow down. This process continues as the coaster car goes through loops, hills, and turns until eventually it comes back to the beginning.

Due to the conservation of energy (the total amount of energy in the system must be conserved), the total amount of kinetic energy and energy lost due to friction can never exceed the initial amount of potential energy the coaster car has. That means roller coaster designers have to make sure the coaster has enough initial potential energy to make it through the rest of the track. This places some limits on the design. For example, the coaster car can't go through a loop or over a hill that is taller than the initial hill because going higher would require more energy than it has available. If the track is too long, friction might eventually cause the coaster car to come to a complete stop. In this project, you will take these factors into consideration as you design your own coaster.

MATERIALS

- Several pieces of paper (Construction paper works well.)
- Tape
- Scissors
- Ruler
- Pencil

- Piece of corrugated cardboard (as large as you would like your roller coaster footprint to be)
- Marble
- Helper (optional)

PREPARATION ····································

- Create segments for your roller coaster track!

- To build a straight track piece: Cut a 3-inch (7.5 cm) strip of paper. Use a ruler and pencil to draw lines that divide it into three, 1-inch (2.5 cm) wide segments. Fold the outer two segments up 90 degrees along these lines.

- To build a loop or a hill track piece: Start with the same steps you used to make a straight piece. Then make marks every inch (2.5 cm) along the two long sides of the paper. Cut inward from these marks to the long lines you drew, forming 1-inch (2.5 cm) square tabs on both sides of the strip. Fold these tabs up 90 degrees. Now you can bend the paper to make hills or loops. Tape the tabs together to make the paper hold its shape. This part can be easier with a helper—one person to hold the paper in place and the other person to do the taping.

- To build a curved track piece: Start with the same steps you used to make a straight piece. Make marks every inch (2.5 cm) along one long edge of the paper. Then make 2-inch (5 cm) cuts inward from these marks. Now fold the uncut side of the paper 90 degrees, and fold the 1-inch (2.5 cm) tabs on the other side up 90 degrees. The bottom portion of this track piece is flexible because it has cuts in it so you can bend it horizontally to form a curve. Tape the tabs together to make the paper hold its shape.

- To build a support strut: Cut a 2.5-inch (6 cm) wide strip of paper. Use a pencil and ruler to draw lines dividing it into five, 0.5-inch (1.3 cm) segments. Crease along these segments and then fold them into a square shape (so two of the segments overlap) and use tape to hold them in place. Make 1-inch (2.5 cm) cuts along the edges from one end, and then fold the resulting tabs outward. This will allow you to tape the tabs flat to a piece of cardboard, so your support strut can stand vertically.

- Make sure all curves, loops, and hills are gradual. Avoid sharp corners or your "roller coaster car" (your marble) might crash and come to an abrupt stop.

PROCEDURE

- Before you start building, plan out a design for your roller coaster. Draw your design on paper, and figure out how many supports and pieces of track you will need. Remember to consider the information in the "Background" section for your design. Make sure your marble starts at the top of a hill!

- Using a piece of corrugated cardboard as a base, assemble your track according to your plan. Tape the track segments together end to end to connect them.

- Place the marble at the top of your track and let it go. Watch carefully. *What happens? Does it make it the whole way through the track?*

- If the marble made it the whole way to the end, try making your track longer by adding more pieces. *How long can you make your track before the marble comes to a stop?*

- If your marble didn't make it to the end, try to figure out why. *Is there a spot in your track where the marble got stuck? Was the marble going too slowly to make it through a loop?* If necessary, make changes to your design, such as making the curves more gradual or the initial hill taller to give the marble more potential energy. Try again. *Can you get your marble to finish the track?*

ExTRA

You can also make roller coasters from foam pipe insulation (available at a hardware store) instead of from paper. This will allow you to make a much bigger coaster more quickly because it doesn't involve as much cutting, folding, and taping.

OBSERVATIONS AND RESULTS ··········

If you followed the guidelines discussed in the "Background" section, you should have been able to design a working roller coaster. Because some energy is always lost to friction, your initial hill needs to be taller than any subsequent hills or loops so the marble has enough energy to make it through. The taller your initial hill, the longer your track can be. If your track had any turns that were too sharp, the marble might have collided with the walls and lost a bunch of energy in the collision. (This energy goes into bending the paper.) That would be painful or even dangerous for the riders if this was a real coaster! That's why it's important to make sure turns are smooth and gradual.

CLEANUP ·················
Recycle the paper and cardboard, and return the other materials to where you found them.

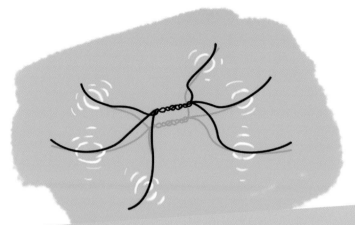

Make Metal Float
Build a Water Strider

BUILD A BUG—THAT FLOATS ON WATER! USE PHYSICS TO FIND OUT HOW THESE INSECTS GLIDE ACROSS PONDS.

Have you ever seen a "water strider" (also called water bugs, pond skaters, water skippers, etc.)? They are bugs that effortlessly hop around on the surface of ponds, lakes, and rivers. How do they do it without sinking? Try this project to find out!

PROJECT TIME

30 to 40 minutes

KEY CONCEPTS

Physics
Forces
Surface tension
Density
Buoyancy

BACKGROUND

If you glance at a water strider, at first you might think it's floating in the water, just like a boat. If you look very closely, however, you'll see it's sitting on top of the water without actually breaking through the surface. How is that possible? It depends on a force called surface tension, which acts on the water strider's legs when they touch the water. Surface tension is a pull at the water's surface that occurs because its molecules are slightly attracted to one another. This property is responsible for many interesting phenomena, such as how bubbles form, how water makes droplets and how plants can suck water out of the ground. In this case, the surface tension creates a thin film, or skin, at the water's surface that is difficult for very small, light objects to break through.

Every object is pulled downward by the force of its own weight. Objects sitting on water can remain above the surface if the upward pull of surface tension is enough to equal the weight. (You might ask, "Wait, how can surface tension pull something up?" or "Wouldn't the water have to push the water strider up to support its weight?" Try the activity and then read the Observations and Results section to find out.) Objects completely or partially submerged in water, such as boats, are pushed up by the buoyant force, which is equal to the weight of the water they displace. If the buoyant force is bigger than the object's weight, it will float. Normally materials that are denser than water (they have more mass per unit volume), such as metals, will sink. Metal boats, however, can float because their hulls are shaped so they displace a lot of water (that is, there is a lot of empty air space inside the boat). In this project, you will make a model water strider out of metal wire and see that you can use surface tension instead of buoyant force to make metal float.

MATERIALS

- Thin wire (You can buy magnet wire or, with permission, cut apart an old cable such as a cell phone charger.)
- Wire strippers or scissors (only needed if you are cutting apart an old cable)
- Shallow tray or bowl
- Water
- An adult helper (if cutting apart an old cable)

PREPARATION

- If you are cutting apart an old cable, have an adult helper use wire strippers to strip off the insulation. The cable might have multiple smaller wires inside it, and those wires might also have insulation. Pull the wires apart and strip off any insulation until you have them down to the bare metal. If you don't have wire strippers, you can ask an adult to carefully use scissors or a sharp knife to scrape off the insulation, but be careful not to cut through the whole wire.

- Fill a shallow tray or bowl with water.

PROCEDURE

- Cut three pieces of wire, each about 3 inches (7.5 cm) to 4 inches (10 cm) long.

- Tightly twist the wires together only in the middle to form your bug's "body." The untwisted ends of the wires should form your bug's six "legs," with three on each side. Spread the legs out to evenly distribute the water strider's weight.

- Curve each of the strider's legs into a long, shallow "U" shape. When you put the water strider down on a flat, solid surface, it should rest evenly on all six legs (that is, none of the legs should be sticking up in the air), with the body up off the ground. Adjust the legs if necessary.

- Gently place your water strider into the tray or bowl of water. *What happens?*

- If your strider sinks, try adjusting its legs. Remember to make sure they're even so all six of them touch the water and the bug's weight is evenly distributed. If one leg goes into the water before the others, all of the strider's weight will be on that leg, and it will probably sink. If it still doesn't float, try adjusting the legs' shapes. You want as much wire to touch the water as possible, so make sure each has a long, very gentle curve and not any sharp bends.

23

- Once you get your wire bug to float, look very closely at where the legs touch the water. *What do you see?*

- Try shaking the bowl or tray to make waves—or sprinkling some water on top of your strider to simulate rain. *What happens?*

⚛ SCIENCE FAIR IDEA

Try adding small weights to your strider (such as tiny bits of tape or paper). *How much weight can you add before it sinks?*

OBSERVATIONS AND RESULTS

You might have had trouble getting your water strider to float at first. It's important to distribute the weight evenly across all six legs, and you should have as much length of the wire touching the water surface as possible. This allows the maximum amount of surface tension to support the bug's weight. If just one leg touches the water first or only a tiny part of each leg touches the water, then all of the bug's weight is concentrated on a small amount of wire, and it will break through the surface.

Once your bug breaks through the surface, it quickly sinks because metal is denser than water. Waves and raindrops can easily break the surface tension and cause your bug to sink. How do real water striders stay afloat when real bodies of water are rarely perfectly still and flat? Their bodies are covered with tiny hairs that trap air bubbles, allowing them to quickly pop back to the surface after submersion.

If you looked very closely at where your bug's legs touched the water, you should have observed they made small dents in the water's surface. This is what enables surface tension to pull up on the legs. Imagine having a bunch of people hold a bedsheet by the edges and pull it tight. The sheet is flat and horizontal so at first it's hard to imagine how it could pull something up. Now imagine tossing a ball into the middle of the sheet. The sheet will sag down slightly but the people pulling on the sheet (creating surface tension) will prevent the ball from sinking deeper into the sheet. Surface tension acts on the water strider's legs in a similar manner.

Finally, if you tried using thicker wire or paper clips to make a strider, it might have been much more difficult—or even impossible! This occurs because surface tension has a relatively stronger effect on very tiny, lightweight objects. That's why water striders are so small and why you can't walk on the surface of water. Even if you try spreading out your arms and legs, you will still break through the surface.

CLEANUP ·

Recycle or throw out the used wire, pour out the water, and return the other materials to where you found them.

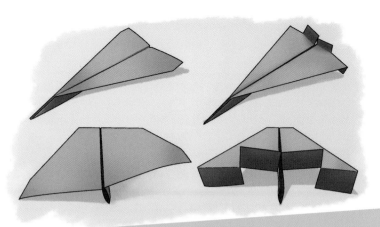

⚛ Soaring Science
Test Paper Planes with Different Drag

TEST OUT AERODYNAMICS WITH
THE CLASSIC PAPER PLANE!

Have you ever wondered what makes a paper plane fly? Some paper planes clearly fly better than others. But why is this? One factor is the kind of design used to build the plane. In this activity, you'll get to build a paper plane and change its basic design to see how this affects its flight. There's a lot of cool science in this activity, such as how forces act on a plane so it can fly. So get ready to start folding!

PROJECT TIME

30 to 40 minutes

KEY CONCEPTS

Aerodynamics
Planes
Forces
Drag
Physics

27

BACKGROUND

The forces that allow a paper plane to fly are the same ones that apply to real airplanes. A force is something that pushes or pulls on something else. When you throw a paper plane in the air, you are giving the plane a push to move forward. That push is a type of force called thrust. While the plane is flying forward, air moving over and under the wings is providing an upward lift force on the plane. At the same time, air pushing back against the plane is slowing it down, creating a drag force. The weight of the paper plane also affects its flight, as gravity pulls it down toward Earth. All of these forces (thrust, lift, drag, and gravity) affect how well a given paper plane's voyage goes. In this activity, you will increase how much drag a paper plane experiences and see if this changes how far the plane flies.

MATERIALS

- Sheet of paper
- Ruler
- Scissors
- Large open area in which to fly a paper plane, such as a long hallway, gym, or basket-ball court. If you're flying your paper plane outside, such as in a field, try to do it when there isn't any wind.
- Something to make a line at least 1 foot (30.5 cm) long, such as a long string, another ruler, masking tape, rocks, or sticks.
- Paper clips (optional)

PREPARATION

- Make a standard, "dart" design paper airplane (for instructions, go to www.amazingpaperairplanes.com/simple-basicdart.html).

- Fold your paper into the basic dart paper plane. Fold carefully and make your folds as sharp as possible, such as by running a thumbnail or a ruler along each fold to crease it.

- Do not bend up the tailing edge of the wings (step 6 of the online folding instructions).

- Go to a large open area and, using string, a ruler, masking tape, rocks, or sticks, make a line in front of you that's at least 1 foot (30.5 cm) long, going from left to right. This will be the starting line from which you'll fly the paper plane.

PROCEDURE ·

- Place your toe on the line you prepared and throw the paper plane. *Did it fly very far?*

- Throw the plane at least four more times. Each time before you throw the plane, make sure it is still in good condition (that the folds and points are still sharp). When you toss it, place your toe on the line and try to launch the plane with a similar amount of force, including gripping it at the same spot. *Did it go about the same distance each time?*

- Once you have a good idea of about how far your plane typically flies, change the plane's shape to increase how much drag it experiences. To do this, cut slits that are about 1 inch (2.5 cm) long right where either wing meets the middle ridge. Fold up the cut section on both wings so that each now has a 1-inch (2.5 cm) wide section at the end of the wing that is folded up, at about a 90-degree angle from the rest of the wing.

- Throw your modified paper plane at least five more times, just as you did before. *How far does the paper plane fly now compared with before? Why do you think this is, and what does it have to do with drag?*

⚛ SCIENCE FAIR IDEA ~~~

Make paper planes that are different sizes and compare how well they fly. *Do bigger planes fly farther?*

SCIENCE FAIR IDEA

Try making paper planes out of different types of paper, such as printer paper, construction paper, and newspaper. Use the same design for each. *Does one type of paper seem to work best for making paper planes? Does one type work the worst?*

 # SCIENCE FAIR IDEA

Some people like to add paper clips to their paper planes to make them fly better. Try adding a paper clip (or multiple paper clips) to different parts of your paper plane (such as the front, back, middle, or wings), and then fly it. *How does this affect the plane's flight? Does adding paper clips somewhere make its flight better or much worse?*

OBSERVATIONS AND RESULTS ··········

Did the original plane fly the farthest? Did the plane with increased drag fly a much shorter distance?

As a paper plane moves through the air, the air pushes against the plane, slowing it down. This force is called drag. To think about drag, imagine you are in a moving car, and you put your hand out the window. The force of the air pushing your hand back as you move forward is drag, also sometimes referred to as air resistance. In this activity, you increased how much drag acted on the paper plane by making a 1-inch (2.5 cm) high vertical strip on both wings. For example, this is what happens when you're in a moving car with your hand out the window and you change its position from horizontal to vertical. When your hand is held out vertically, it catches a greater amount of air and experiences a greater drag than when it is horizontal. You could probably feel this, as your hand would be more forcefully pushed back as the car moves forward. This is what happened to the modified plane—it experienced a greater amount of drag, which pushed it back more than the original plane. This experiment has clearly demonstrated that altering how just one force acts on a paper plane can dramatically change how well it flies.

CLEANUP ··········

Recycle the paper plane when you are done with it.

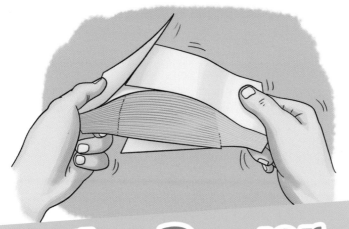

The Power of Friction

CAN YOU PULL APART TWO SMALL BOOKS? THE ANSWER MIGHT SURPRISE YOU! LEARN HOW FRICTION CAN MULTIPLY AS YOU STACK ON THE PAGES. IT MIGHT JUST KEEP YOU TUGGING!

Sometimes friction can be annoying. It can make it difficult to push heavy things like furniture and it can even give you a nasty scrape if you fall. But friction is actually very important—without it, you could not move around at all, or even pick things up! Try this project to find out how friction can lead to some surprising effects—such as making it almost impossible to pull two books apart.

PROJECT TIME
15 to 20 minutes

KEY CONCEPTS
Physics
Forces
Friction
Surface area

BACKGROUND

You experience friction every day. When you walk, friction is what prevents your feet from slipping on the floor. Imagine if every surface were as slippery as ice—getting around would be very difficult! Friction is a type of force, or a "push" or a "pull," that can act on objects.

In physics, the frictional force between two surfaces is determined by something called the coefficient of friction. A higher coefficient of friction means that there will be more friction between two surfaces, or they will be less "slippery." For example, the rubber soles of your shoes and a carpeted floor have a much higher coefficient than ice skates on ice. The amount of friction also depends on something called the normal force. In this context, "normal" means "perpendicular to the surface." A higher normal force will result in higher friction. For example, imagine two identical cardboard boxes sitting on a wooden floor. One box is empty and very light, and one is full of stuff and very heavy. In both cases, the coefficient of friction (between cardboard and wood) is the same. The heavier box, however, will be much harder to slide across the floor. This is because there is a higher normal force between the box and the floor, so there is more friction.

Now, think about friction between two pieces of paper. If you put two pieces of paper on top of one another, they should be very easy to pull apart, right? What will happen if you overlap a whole bunch of pieces of paper, like the pages from two books? Will they still be easy to pull apart? Try this surprising activity to find out!

MATERIALS

- Two equal-size books (such as phone books) or two thick magazines, notepads, or tablets of sticky notes.

PREPARATION

- Take your two books or notepads and place them on a flat table so the "bound" ends are facing away from one another.

PROCEDURE

- Open both books and overlap their back covers at least halfway.

- One by one interleave the pages of the two books by folding down a page from the left book then a page from the right book on top of that, and then a page from the left book again.

- Continue alternating in this fashion for about a dozen pages.

- Now try to pull the books apart. *How easy is it to pull the books apart? Can you do it? What if you hang the books vertically by holding on to just one of them—can they support their own weight?*

- Start over and interleave more pages than you did the first time.

- Repeat the testing process, trying different tests to see if you can pull the books apart. *Can the books hold their own weight if you hang them vertically? Can you do "tug of war" with another person to pull them apart?*

- Continue performing the tests after interleaving more and more pages until you can no longer pull the books apart. *Are you surprised at how much force the books can support? How many pages did you have to interleave before you could no longer pull them apart?*

- To separate the books, you might have to fold the pages back one at a time. You can also try bending the two books relative to one another, which will cause the pages at one end of the stack to start coming apart.

ExTRA

Try the activity with two notepads or notebooks that have perforated, removable sheets. Remove every other sheet of paper from each notebook, then try the different tests. *Are they just as difficult to pull apart, or does something change? Why do you think that might be?*

OBSERVATIONS AND RESULTS ··········

You should have found that it was pretty easy to pull the books apart when only several pages were interleaved. As you interleave more and more pages, however, it quickly becomes surprisingly difficult to pull them apart—until pretty soon, you cannot separate them at all! Although the classical demonstration of this project uses large phone books, it works well even for much tinier volumes, including sticky note pads. Can you figure out why this happens, based on what you read in the Background section?

You know that the coefficient of friction does not change, because the surfaces remain the same material (paper). It turns out that when you try to pull the two books apart, the interleaved pages in the middle get squished together harder—this increases the normal force between them, thereby increasing overall friction. This means that the harder you pull, the higher the friction, and the harder the pages are to pull apart!

There are many demonstrations and videos of this project online but be careful when you read about it because there are several common misconceptions and incorrect explanations for how it works. One misconception is that the effect is due to the normal force from the weight of all the pages pressing down on one another. This cannot be true, however, because the activity still works if you hang the books vertically, in which case there is no normal force from the weight of each page acting on the next page. The second common incorrect explanation is that the "increased surface area" from interleaving many pages together results in more friction. This is also incorrect—a regular stack of paper will easily fall apart, even though there is lots of surface area in contact between the sheets. The effect in this activity occurs because the interleaved sheets in the middle get squeezed together as you try to pull the books apart. You can see this if you look at your books edge-on while you do the experiment. When you are not pulling on them at all—or even if you push them together a little bit—you should be able to see some small gaps between some of the pages. But when you pull on the books, these gaps quickly close and the pages flatten together. Try the "extra" step in the procedure to see how this changes if you use notepads with every other page removed. (This results in the stack of interleaved pages in the middle being the same height as the binding of either notepad, instead of twice as thick—so the pages are not pulled inward when you try to pull them apart.)

CLEANUP ··················

Return the books to where you found them.

Slippery Science
Explore Friction by Launching Stuff

SLIP AND SLIDE WITH THIS ACTIVITY TO DETERMINE HOW MUCH FRICTION SURFACES HAVE.

PROJECT TIME
 20 to 30 minutes

KEY CONCEPTS

Physics
Friction
Motion
Materials

Have you ever tried to get a running start and slide across a smooth, wooden floor while wearing socks? What happens if you try the same thing on a carpeted floor or while wearing shoes? The amount of friction between your feet and the floor surface determines how well you can slide. Some combinations of surfaces, such as socks on a wooden floor, produce very little friction. Other combinations, such as rubber soles on a wooden floor, produce much more friction. In this project, you'll do a much smaller-scale friction experiment by launching tiny objects along a surface with a rubber band. How do you think friction will affect how far the objects slide?

37

BACKGROUND

Friction is the force that opposes motion between two surfaces that are touching one another. Friction is a very important part of everyday life—without it, you wouldn't be able to walk because your feet would just slip on the floor! Sometimes it is very important for surfaces to have high friction, such as the rubber tires of a car on the road. Other times, we want surfaces to have low friction, such as when you go down a slide at the playground or sled on a snowy hill. The amount of friction changes depending on which materials come into contact with one another.

Another thing that can affect friction on an object is the object's weight. Imagine pushing two boxes—one heavier than the other—made out of the same material. You will have to push harder to move the heavier box. This is because gravity pulls down harder on the heavier one, which increases its friction with the floor. In this experiment, you will keep the weight of the objects you use constant so that you can test different materials without worrying about gravity's effects.

MATERIALS

- Rubber band
- Stack of five or six quarters
- Scotch tape
- Smooth wooden surface, such as a table or floor (If you do not have a wooden surface, you can use any other type of smooth countertop or table.)
- Rough carpeted surface (If you do not have access to carpet, you can tape down several paper towels on top of your smooth surface.)
- Ruler (optional)

PREPARATION

- Stack your quarters on top of one another. Wrap them in tape so they are secured together. Make sure the bottom of the stack is smooth, with no sharp corners of tape sticking out. (These could get caught on the carpet.)

- Make sure the wooden and carpeted surfaces you will work with are free from any other objects or obstructions.

PROCEDURE •

- Form a "C" shape with your index finger and your thumb.

- Carefully stretch the rubber band between your index finger and thumb to form a slingshot.

- Still carefully holding the rubber band, turn your hand upside-down and touch the tips of your finger and thumb to the wooden surface so the rubber band rests just above the surface.

- Load the stack of quarters into your slingshot and pull back on the rubber band. Pay attention to how far you pull back the rubber band; it is important to pull back the same amount each time. *What do you think will happen when you release the quarters?*

- Let go of the quarters to launch them. Watch closely to make sure they slide across the wood and do not get launched into the air or tumble. If the quarters don't slide smoothly, adjust your rubber band and try again.

- Repeat the launch several times and watch how far the quarters go. Remember to make sure you pull the rubber band back the same distance each time. *Do the quarters slide very far, or do they come to a stop quickly? What do you think this tells you about friction between your stack of quarters and the wooden surface?*

- Now, repeat the same process on the carpet. Be careful not to let any corners of the tape get stuck on the carpet. *How far do the quarters go on carpet? Do they go farther or less far than they did on wood? What does this tell you about friction between the stack of quarters and the carpet? Is it higher or lower than on wood?*

ExTRA

Use a ruler to record how far the quarters go each time. Record all your results in a table and then calculate an average distance for each surface. *How far do the quarters go on average for the wood surface? How far do they go on average for the carpet?*

 ## SCIENCE FAIR IDEA

Try out more test surfaces in addition to wood and carpet. *What if you go outside and try the experiment on a hard, rough surface, such as the sidewalk or driveway? What about other surfaces you can find in your home? How far do the quarters slide on different surfaces? Can you guess whether a surface will have high or low friction just by looking at it?*

 ## SCIENCE FAIR IDEA

Repeat the activity using different objects instead of your stack of quarters. *For example, how do your results change if you try the experiment with a large rubber pencil eraser?* Remember that an object's weight determines how much friction it will encounter, so try to use objects that are about the same weight. (You can use a kitchen scale to weigh different objects.) *Can you find an object that always slides farther than the quarters? What about one that always doesn't slide as far?*

OBSERVATIONS AND RESULTS ··········

Did the quarters go farther on the smooth wooden surface or on the carpet?

You should have found that the quarters went much farther on the smooth wooden surface than they did on the carpet. Depending on the strength of your rubber band and how far back you pulled it, you might even have launched them all the way off the table or countertop! This occurs because there is much more friction between the stack of quarters and the carpet's rough surface than there is between them and the smooth surface of the wood. Because there is less friction slowing them down, the quarters can slide farther on the wood before they eventually come to a stop.

CLEANUP ···············

Remove the tape from the quarters and throw it away. Put away the quarters and other items where you found them.

Steering Science
Make a Homemade Compass

MAKE YOUR VERY OWN COMPASS WITH JUST A NEEDLE, CORK, AND A LITTLE ELBOW GREASE!

Have you used a compass to help you figure out what direction you should go? These can come in handy to help you navigate your way through a field or forest while camping, for example. Magnetic compasses work based on Earth's magnetic field. In this science activity, you'll get to make your own magnetic compass. How well do you think it'll work? Get ready to find out!

PROJECT TIME
20 to 30 minutes

KEY CONCEPTS
Magnetism
Navigation
Magnetic poles
Physics
Forces

43

BACKGROUND

People have known about magnetism for thousands of years. Magnetism is the reason two magnets will push against one another or be pulled together. This can cause amazing things to happen, such as making an object hover above the ground because it is being pushed up by the magnetic force. Magnetism can also help people navigate; because Earth has a magnetic field, compasses can be made using a small magnetized bar or needle that points a certain direction (north or south) based on the field.

Although the phenomenon of magnetism has been known for a couple thousand years, the first magnetic compasses used for navigation were not invented until relatively recently, approximately 1,000 years ago (sometime between 1000 and 1100 CE). In this science activity, you'll get to make your own compass, which may help you understand some of the challenges that early magnetic compass makers encountered!

MATERIALS

- Metal sewing needle
- A magnet (It can be a flat refrigerator magnet or a more powerful magnet, such as a rare earth magnet—the most common type is made of neodymium—which can be purchased at many hardware stores. A stronger magnet will work best.)
- A pair of pliers
- A cork
- Scissors for cutting the cork
- A wide cup, drinking glass or bowl
- Water

PREPARATION

- Be careful when handling the magnet, especially if you are using a strong magnet, such as a rare earth magnet. Keep the magnet away from other magnets and electronic devices, such as computers, cell phones, and TV screens.

44

- Use caution and have an adult help when you use the scissors to cut the cork and when you handle the needle.

PROCEDURE ....

- Rub the magnet against the sewing needle at least five times. (If you are using a weaker magnet, such as a flat refrigerator magnet, rub the needle at least a dozen times.) Always rub the magnet in the same direction against the needle. Your needle should now be magnetized.

- Now cut off about 0.25 inch (6 mm) of the cork from one of the ends, making a small cork disk that is about 0.25-inch (6 mm) tall.

- Laying the cork disk on a flat surface, carefully push the needle through the side of the disk by using the pair of pliers. Push the needle all the way through the disk so that about the same amount of needle shows on either side of the disk.

- Fill a wide cup, drinking glass or bowl with at least 1 inch (2.5 cm) of water.

- Put the cork disk (with the needle) on the water in the cup. Try to keep the disk floating in the center of the water, away from the sides of the cup. *What does the needle do? When it stops moving, what direction does it point toward?*

- *Does your homemade compass seem to work well? How is it limited in its use?*

ExTRA

Find out what direction north is in your location. *Did your needle point in that direction?* (You can use a real compass, an atlas, or smartphone map for this.)

EXTRA

Put a magnet next to your compass. *What happens to the needle as the magnet is moved close to it? How close does the magnet need to be to affect the compass?* You could also try this with a steel object (such as a nail or possibly the pliers).

⚛ SCIENCE FAIR IDEA

If you have magnets with different strengths, such as a flat refrigerator magnet and a rare earth magnet, try making multiple compasses using the different magnets to magnetize the needles. *How well do the different compasses work compared with one another?*

EXTRA

There are other ways you can make an inexpensive magnetic compass at home or while you are outdoors. For example, instead of using a piece of cork, you could try using a small leaf and setting the needle on top of the leaf while it floats in a still pool of water. *How does a compass made using a leaf compare with one made using a piece of cork? How else could you make a magnetic compass?*

OBSERVATIONS AND RESULTS ··········

Did the needle in your homemade compass align itself along Earth's north and south poles?

When you rubbed the magnet against the sewing needle, you magnetized the needle, effectively making it a weak, temporary magnet. Because magnets interact with one another (pushing against one another or pulling one another together), the magnetized needle can interact with Earth's magnetic field. Although Earth's magnetic field is relatively weak, it should have clearly affected the needle because the needle was allowed to freely float in the cork disk on the water. Specifically, once it stopped moving, the needle should have aligned itself along Earth's magnetic field, lining up along the north/south axis.

This means that one end of the needle should have pointed north, while the other pointed south. The same end should have always pointed the same direction. (You can do some more research to figure out how to make a compass that always has the needle's tip point a specific direction—either north or south.)

CLEANUP • • • • • • • • • • • • • • • • • • •

Pour out the water, recycle the cork, and put away the other items where you found them.

A Really Long Straw

WHY AREN'T THERE MORE SUPER-LONG STRAWS? LEARN HOW YOUR MOUTH "VACUUMS" UP BEVERAGES WHEN YOU SIP THROUGH A STRAW—AND BUILD YOUR OWN MEGA STRAW TO LEARN ABOUT THE PHYSICS BEHIND THIS IMPRESSIVE EVERYDAY FEAT! HOW LONG CAN YOU GO?

Have you ever used a crazy straw? Some spiral their way up. Others have fancy colors or decorations. Some are thin and others are wide. But just about all of them leave you sipping your drink from about the same distance. Why? Wouldn't it be fun to poke your head out of an upstairs window and secretly take a sip from a drink way below? Would it even be possible? With this activity, you'll see if you can set your own record for the longest working straw!

PROJECT TIME

30 to 45 minutes

KEY CONCEPTS

Pressure
Atmospheric pressure
Air pressure
Gravity

BACKGROUND

Sipping a drink through a straw might seem simple. But you are actually using some fancy air pressure changes to move your beverage. The sipping action occurs when you lower the air pressure in your mouth, which allows the atmospheric pressure to push the liquid up the straw.

Does that sound bizarre? Here is a little more explanation: The atmosphere is a massive layer of air. The weight of all that air is constantly pressing on us and on the things around us. At sea level, this invisible pressure is approximately 14.7 pounds per square inch. That is like having the weight of a bowling ball sitting on each square inch or five bowling balls pressing on the liquid filling a glass with a 2.5 inch diameter (6.4 cm). Put a straw into liquid, and the liquid will enter the straw until it reaches the same level as the liquid outside the straw. The liquid in the straw and around it is being pushed down by the air above it in a similar way, so they reach about the same level.

But it gets interesting when you remove some air from the straw. Suddenly, there is less air pressure inside and liquid is pushed up the straw. The more air you remove from the straw, the higher the liquid will be pushed into it.

Do you think there is a limit to how high the liquid can rise in a straw? This activity will help you make a very large "mega-straw" and test it out!

MATERIALS

- A package of plastic straws (at least one dozen), preferably those with a bendable part
- Scissors
- Ruler
- Tape
- Drinking glass filled with water
- Level surface that can get wet (or if not, something to protect your surface)
- Sturdy chair or table on which to stand

PREPARATION

- Have an adult help to cut two 0.5-inch (1.3 cm) slits, across from one another, lengthwise in one end of a plastic straw. These cuts will help you slip the end of one straw over another one.

- Prepare 10 more straws in a similar way until you have enough for a superlong mega-straw! (You can also come back to these steps during the process in case you need more straws for your mega-straw.)

PROCEDURE •••••••••••••••••••••••••••••••••••••

- Slip the cut end of a prepared straw over the end of an unprepared straw.

- Wrap the area where the straws overlap with tape so you have an airtight seal. Do not hurry; a good airtight seal will help you avoid trouble later. *Why do you think a secure, airtight seal is essential for your mega-straw to function well?* (**Hint:** When you drink with a straw, you must remove air from it.)

- To test your extralong straw, put a glass of water on level ground. (Be sure to place something down to protect your level surface or use one that can get wet.) Now hold your straw vertically or close to vertically and try to drink with it. *Does water reach your mouth?*

- If little or no liquid enters the straw, check the seal where you joined the straws. *Is it airtight?* If not, add tape or undo and redo this connection. If the seals at all joints seem airtight, check for holes in other areas of your mega-straw and seal them with tape.

- Play around with your first mega-straw. Suck lightly to remove a little air from the straw then suck hard to remove more air. Observe each time how high the water rises in your mega-straw. *What happens if you suck up more air? Why do you think this happens?*

- Time to add on! Attach another prepared straw to your mega-straw in a similar way and put your lengthened mega-straw to the test. Remember to hold your straw vertically or close to vertically during your test. *Is your new straw functioning properly? Does it get harder to suck up water?*

- Keep adding prepared straws and testing after each addition. You might have to carefully stand on a chair to test your growing mega-straw. *Does it become harder and harder to suck up water as you stand higher and higher above the glass?*

- Once you have connected a few straws together and it is a little challenging to drink with the straw, test your mega-straw at different angles. In addition to holding the straw vertically, test it at an angle about halfway between horizontal and vertical (approximately 45 degrees) as well as by holding it as close to horizontal as possible. Note that you might need to add more water to your glass to test a fairly horizontal position. *Is there a difference in effort needed to suck up water?* If so, rank the straw positions in descending order: 1 being the hardest to suck up water, or needing the most effort; 3 being the easiest, or needing the least effort. Note that you did not change the distance over which the water was transported; the straw stayed the same length. *What did you change that might have created a difference in effort needed?*

- Pause a moment and think about how the difference in height between your mouth and the glass changed depending on the angle at which you held the mega-straw. Rank the methods in descending order of difference in height between your mouth and the glass: 1 being the position with the most height; 3, the position with the least height. *Do you see a correlation between the difference in height and the effort you needed to suck up water?*

- If you have bendable sections in your straw, test what happens if you keep the height of your glass and your head the same but change the way you bend the mega-straw. Try a straight mega-straw and a mega-straw with one or several kinks. *How do the levels of effort compare now that you keep the difference in height unchanged?*

- Build on. *How many straws can you connect before you can no longer drink from it if held vertically? Do you think there is a limit or would you be able to build on indefinitely, as long as you could test it from higher and higher places?*

OBSERVATIONS AND RESULTS • • • • • • • • •

When you suck air from the straw, less air pushes on the water inside the straw than on the water outside of it. This imbalance causes more water to be pushed into the straw. The water will rise until the pressure created by the water column in the straw equals the air pressure difference.

Remove more air, and a bigger difference in air pressure will cause the water level to rise even higher into the straw. As soon as the water reaches the height of your mouth, you can drink.

Your lung power determines how much air you can remove. Some people will have difficulty with a 3-foot (0.9 m) straw whereas others can successfully drink standing 8 feet (2.4 m) above their drink!

There is a limit though. If you could create a complete vacuum in your mouth by removing all the air, the water could rise about 30 feet (9.1 m) high. It's not possible, however, to create a complete vacuum in the human mouth, so usually people reach their straw-slurping limit at a much lower level!

Note that it is mainly the difference in height the water needs to overcome that counts, not the total length the water needs to travel in the straw. Holding your straw almost horizontally will allow you to suck up water over a very long distance.

CLEANUP • • • • • • • • • • • • • • • • • • •

Pour out the water, throw away the used straws, and put away other materials.

Showing Science
Watch Objects in Free Fall

RE-CREATE GALILEO GALILEI'S EXPERIMENT TESTING HOW FAST DIFFERENT OBJECTS FALL DUE TO EARTH'S GRAVITY.

Have you ever wondered how fast a heavy object falls compared with a lighter one? Imagine if you dropped both of them at the same time. Which would hit the ground first? Would it be the heavier one because it weighs more? Or would they hit the ground at the same time? In the late 1500s in Italy, the famous scientist Galileo was asking some of these same questions. And he did some experiments to answer them. In this activity, you'll do some of your own tests to determine whether heavier objects fall faster than lighter ones.

PROJECT TIME

20 to 30 minutes

KEY CONCEPTS

Physics
Free fall
Forces
Gravity
Mass
Inertia

55

BACKGROUND

In 4th-century BCE Greece, the philosopher Aristotle theorized that the speed at which an object falls is probably relative to its mass. In other words, if two objects are the same size but one is heavier, the heavier one has greater density than the lighter object. Therefore, when both objects are dropped from the same height and at the same time, the heavier object should hit the ground before the lighter one. Is this true?

Some 1,800 years later, in late 16th-century Italy, the young scientist and mathematician Galileo Galilei questioned Aristotle's theories of falling objects. He even performed several experiments to test Aristotle's theories. As legend has it, in 1589 Galileo stood on a balcony near the top of the Tower of Pisa and dropped two balls that were the same size but had different densities. Although there is debate about whether this actually happened, the story emphasizes the importance of using experimentation to test scientific theories, even ones that had been accepted for nearly 2,000 years.

MATERIALS

- Two balls of the same size, but different mass. For example, you could use a metal and a rubber ball or a wooden and a plastic ball, as long as the two balls are about the same size. If two spherical balls like this are unavailable, you could try something like an apple and a similarly sized round rock.

- A ladder or step stool
- A video camera and a helper (optional)

PREPARATION

- You will be dropping the two balls from the same height, at the same time. Set up the ladder or step stool where you will do your test. If you are using a heavy ball, be sure to find a testing area where the ball will not hurt the floor or ground when it lands.

- If you are using a video camera to record the experiment, set up the camera now and have your helper get ready to record.

- Be careful when using the step stool or ladder.

PROCEDURE

- Carefully climb the ladder or step stool with the two balls.

- Drop both balls at the same time, from the same height. If you are using a video camera, be sure to have your helper record the balls falling and hitting the ground.

- *Did one ball hit the ground before the other or did both balls hit the ground at the same time?*

- Repeat the experiment at least two more times. *Are your results consistent? Did one ball consistently hit the ground before the other or did both balls always hit the ground at the same time?*

- If you videotaped your experiments, you can watch the recordings to verify your results.

- *Can you explain your results?*

 SCIENCE FAIR IDEA

Try this experiment again but this time use balls that have the same mass but are different sizes. *Does one ball hit the ground before the other or do they hit it at the same time?*

 SCIENCE FAIR IDEA

Try testing two objects that have the same mass, but are different shapes. For example, you could try a large feather and a very small ball. *Does one object hit the ground before the other or do they hit it at the same time?*

EXTRA

Try this experiment again but record it using a camera that lets you play back the recording in slow motion. *If you watch the balls falling in slow motion, what do you notice about how they are falling over time? Are both objects always falling at the same speed or is one falling faster than the other at certain points in time?*

OBSERVATIONS AND RESULTS •••••••••

Did both balls hit the ground at the same time?

You should have found that both balls hit the ground at roughly the same time. According to legend, this is what Galileo showed in 1589 from his Tower of Pisa experiment but, again, it's debated whether this actually happened. If you neglect air resistance, objects falling near Earth's surface fall with the same approximate acceleration of 32.17 feet per second squared (9.8 m/s², or g) due to Earth's gravity. So the acceleration is the same for the objects, and consequently their velocity is also increasing at a constant rate. Because the downward force on an object is equal to its mass multiplied by g, heavier objects have a greater downward force. Heavier objects, however, also have more inertia, which means they resist moving more than lighter objects do, and so heavier objects need more force to get them going at the same rate.

CLEANUP ••••••
Put away all materials.

THE SCIENTIFIC METHOD

The scientific method helps scientists—and students—gather facts to prove whether an idea is true. Using this method, scientists come up with ideas and then test those ideas by observing facts and drawing conclusions. You can use the scientific method to develop and test your own ideas!

Question: What do you want to learn? What problem needs to be solved? Be as specific as possible.

Research: Learn more about your topic and refine your question.

Hypothesis: Form an educated guess about what you think will answer your question. This allows you to make a prediction you can test.

Experiment: Create a test to learn if your hypothesis is correct. Limit the number of variables, or elements of the experiment that could change.

Analysis: Record your observations about the progress and results of your experiment. Then analyze your data to understand what it means.

Conclusion: Review all your data. Did the results of the experiment match the prediction? If so, your hypothesis was correct. If not, your hypothesis may need to be changed.

GLOSSARY

accelerate: To increase in speed.

aerodynamic: Having a shape that allows air to flow easily around something so it can move faster.

approximate: Almost correct or exact.

atmosphere: The mixture of gases that surround a planet.

buoyant: Able to stay afloat in liquid or gas.

centripetal: Moving toward the center.

coefficient: In physics, something that measures a property.

collide: To crash two objects against one another.

diameter: The distance from one side of a round object to another through its center.

linear: Relating to a straight line.

magnetic field: The area around a magnet where its pull is felt. Also, the area near a planet where magnetic forces can be found. Earth has a magnetic field.

perpendicular: Being at right angles.

phenomenon: A fact or an event that is observed.

propel: To cause to move or push.

seismograph: A machine that detects and records earthquakes.